Launch Into Reading Success

Book II

Lorna Bennett
Pamela Ottley

Units of Sound (Advanced)	Rhyme (Advanced)
Onset and Rime (Advanced)	Discrimination of Middle Sounds
Analysis and Synthesis of Phonemes	Linkage
Integration of Sounds	Plays

Order this book online at www.trafford.com
or email orders@trafford.com

Most Trafford titles are also available at major online book retailers.

Printed in the United States of America.

ISBN: 978-1-4251-8809-2 (sc)

Trafford rev. 05/06/2011

 www.trafford.com

North America & international
toll-free: 1 888 232 4444 (USA & Canada)
phone: 250 383 6864 ♦ fax: 812 355 4082

Table of Contents

INTRODUCTION

Tell me, I'll forget. Show me and I may remember. But involve me and I'll understand.
— *Asian Proverb*

FEATURES

LAUNCH INTO READING SUCCESS: THROUGH PHONOLOGICAL AWARE-NESS TRAINING (Book I) offered classroom and learning assistance teachers a thorough, sequenced auditory training program to use with Kindergarten or Grade One children.

LAUNCH INTO READING SUCCESS BOOK II now offers advanced lessons in Awareness of Whole Words as Units of Sound; Rhyme; Onset and Rime, Discrimination of Middle Sounds, and Analysis and Synthesis of Phonemes as an auditory training program for grade one (or some grade two) children.

In addition, it provides three extensive new sections to train phonics skills and reading fluency: Linkage, Integration of Sounds, and Plays.

This program is particularly useful for teachers working with grade one children who are at risk for reading difficulty.

It will be of great value to teachers working with grade two children who appear to have severe problems with early reading skills.

Like Book I, Book II is a teacher-friendly program requiring only minimal extra adult time that could be through the use of teacher assistants and/or parents under the teacher's supervision.

i

The Eight Sections

- provide **79 activity lessons** for the teacher,

- are sequentially developed providing a clear and rich amount of practice at each stage,

- contain stated **learning outcomes and resources**,

- give special attention to **explicit linkage**, word automaticity and **reading fluency**, and

- are very **activity-oriented**.

The Student Record Sheets

- offer assessment over time.

- provide teachers with individual and group record forms (see the Appendix), and

- pinpoint the areas where a child needs more help and the specific type of help needed.

RATIONALE

Many children at-risk for reading difficulties continue to need daily extra teaching of phonological processing skills in grade one. Such reaching will increase the effectiveness of regular grade one reading teaching (Torgesen and Rashotte, 2001).

Research studies have also shown that children at-risk for reading difficulties need very direct, explicit and intense teaching of phonic skills during grade one (Foorman, Francis, Mehta, Schatschneider, Fletcher, 1998; Torgesen, Wagner, Rashotte, Rose, Lindamood, Conway and Garvan, 1999; Vellutino, Scalon, Sipay, Small, Pratt, Chen and Denckla, 1996).

Word automaticity and reading fluency are separate but important areas to be taught in grade one. Therefore, sections on automaticity at the word level and reading fluency at the sentence level are included. They are of crucial importance to reading comprehension and the enjoyment of books.

Launch Into Reading Success Book II provides phonological skills training, phonics teaching, word automaticity and reading fluency exercises. IT provides intense, systematic and explicit teaching that is easy to deliver.

BIOGRAPHY

Lorna Bennett, Ph.D., has thirty years experience teaching kindergarten through university. In 1986, Lorna was recognized by her colleagues with the David Kendall Master teacher award. As a teacher of teachers, she has conducted extensive professional training throughout British Columbia on program modification and the inclusion of learning-disabled children.

Lorna established a District-based Diagnostic Center and implemented ongoing support for children with learning problems.

Lorna has been a member of a Canadian team of teachers, sponsored by the British Columbia Teachers' Federation and the Canadian Teachers' Federation, to teach educators in Guyana (1991) and Thailand (1993). Lorna has conducted workshops for teachers in the USA (Minnisota, Seattle, San Diego, New Orleans and Florida) and in Karachi, Pakistan. She has worked with educators in Pakistan (2000) and Belize (2002, 2003).

Lorna retired in 2003 as a School Psychologist from School District 44 (North Vancouver, British Columbia). She is currently an Educational Consultant in Private Practice in West Vancouver.

Pamela Ottley, Ph.D., is an educational psychologist who studied at University College, London, Brooks College, Oxford, and the University of British Columbia. She has many years of experience as a psychologist in the U.K. and Canada in both the public and private sectors.

Pam began to provide workshops on early screening and intervention in England before the first commercial tests were available. She also co-wrote an intervention program that became used throughout Hampshire schools. She continued to make presentations on this subject as both screening and intervention methods became more numerous and widely available: in the UK, the USA and Canada.

Currently Pam is an independent educational consultant, providing assessment and consultancy services to students teachers and parents and also offering workshops and training for teachers and parents.

As well as being co-author of "Launch Into Reading Success: Through Phonological Awareness Training", she has written "Sound Track for Reading" (Vancouver CA: LEARNING SOLUTIONS).

.

TERMINOLOGY

PHONOLOGY	• The system of (spoken) language which relates meanings and sounds • A study of the sound system of languages • Development of (a child's) speech sounds
PHONOLOGICAL AWARENESS	• Conscious access to the sound structure of words
PHONEMES	• The smallest units of sound that can affect meaning (within a word) • 26 letters but 44 phonemes because of dual usage (e.g. "**c**" as in *cat* and "**c**" as in *cell*), and digraphs (e.g., *ship* and *chip*).
ONSET AND RIME	• The first sound in a one-syllable word (e.g., **m** in *main*) is the onset. • The remainder of the one-syllable word (e.g., **ain** in *main*) is the rime.
WORD AUTOMATICITY	• Fast, accurate and effortless word identification at the single word level.
READING FLUENCY	• Word automaticity plus the application of appropriate prosodic features (rhythm, intonation and phrasing) at the phrase, sentence and text levels.

VITAL ANSWERS
TO VITAL QUESTIONS

How Do We Know Which Children Need Ongoing Phonological Awareness Training?

Launch Into Reading Success Book I record sheets will indicate which children need ongoing phonological skills training. Alternatively, grade one tests of phonological skills could be used to identify children still at-risk of reading difficulties at the end of Kindergarten.

These tests have been found to be successful in finding at least 80% of children at risk of reading difficulty, many of which would not be selected in other ways. However, experienced teachers who have concerns about other children are urged to include them in the intervention group.

How Is Phonological Awareness Different from Phonics and How Is It Related to Whole Language?

This training stands outside the 'Phonics versus Whole Language' debate. Phonological awareness is different from phonic skills, and it is very important to understand the difference between the two processes.

Phonological awareness training aims to give children conscious access to the sounds within words. It is primarily auditory training and is very activity oriented. Sounds of words are introduced and reinforced utilizing a variety of strategies such as tapping, clapping, rhyme schemes, games, etc.

Phonic instruction, however, is a different stage and process to phonological awareness training. Phonic instruction provides knowledge of letter-to-sound correspondence so that children can encode and decode; this strategy tends to involve some paper-and-pencil exercises.

'Whole Language' approaches are essential. Children always need a rich source of literature in supported situations, such as looking, sharing, paired reading and being read to, which emphasizes the meaning of language as opposed to its form. This strategy should continue parallel to phonological awareness training.

Where and When Should it Be Done?

Launch Into Reading Success Book II will remain great fun as a daily short activity! The authors believe that the best place to work is a quiet corner of the classroom. This prevents any message that the selected group is labelled or have special needs.

The time of day will be set mainly by the practicalities facing the teacher. However, it would be unwise to do this program towards the end of the afternoon when children are tired.

What Do I Say to Parents?

Phonological awareness training, when provided at an early age, will help your child be better prepared for reading and spelling. This training will help your child to develop better listening skills and to hear distinctly the sounds within spoken words. However phonics skills, word automaticity and reading fluency are separate and important areas to be taught in grade one.

How Do I Use the Program?

Identify a time in the day when this group of children can work with yourself or with a teacher aide or parent volunteer. The session should run for approximately 30 minutes (sometimes a little less, but very rarely more).

The session plans, and the steps outlined, should be followed <u>sequentially</u>.

It is important to keep a record of group and individual progress, using the convenient record sheets (see the Appendix). These sheets can be used to note any difficulties a child may have as the teaching progresses. This will become a valuable assessment for future teaching and for enlisting some parental support if necessary.

How much time is involved?

Launch Into Reading Success Book II requires a maximum of 30 minutes daily for each lesson.

The classroom teacher can teach the group while the rest of the class is occupied and supervised by another staff member. Sometimes the lesson will be done by a teacher aide or parent volunteer who is working closely under your supervision.

Obviously there will be unusual days when the whole timetable changes and the lesson cannot be done at all. However, try as much as possible to maintain consistent daily input because the program was designed in this manner. Longer sessions, twice a week, are not advised.

THE SEQUENCED SECTIONS OF BOOK II

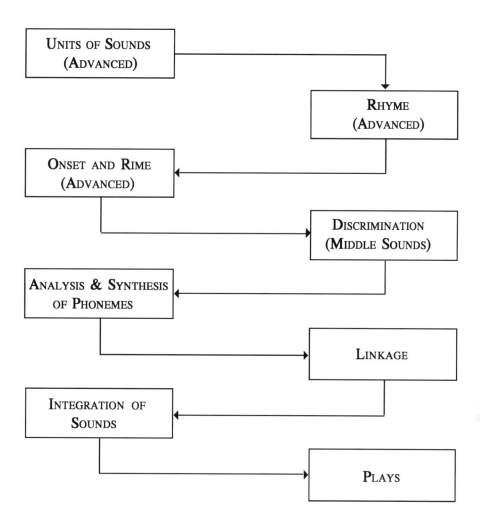

AWARENESS OF WHOLE WORDS
AS UNITS OF SOUND (ADVANCED)

Activity 1

Aim: To consolidate the children's recognition of words as separate units of sound.

Learning Outcome:

Children will respond accurately to three, four or five-word strings by moving cubes (or counters) into three, four or five boxes.

Materials: Fig. 1 — A five-square grid per child
Fig. 2 — List of sentences

Method:

1. Give out the cubes (counters) and a five-square grid to each child.

2. Explain that the children move a counter into a square (from left to right) for each word of the three, four or five-word string.

3. Say this sentence as a practice and tell the children that you will only say it once, so they must listen very carefully — *"It is hot."*

4. Check that each child moved three cubes into each of three separate boxes of the grid.

5. If anyone hesitated, repeat the item to allow everyone to succeed.

6. Use all the remaining nineteen sentences from Fig. 2

   There are enough items to allow group and individual response. Let each child make one individual response.

AWARENESS OF WHOLE WORDS
AS UNITS OF SOUND (ADVANCED)

Fig. 1

AWARENESS OF WHOLE WORDS AS UNITS OF SOUND (ADVANCED)

Fig. 2

LIST OF SENTENCES FOR ACTIVITY 1

It is hot.

Shall we go out?

Come and play with me.

Play in the park.

How are you, Sam?

Mom is here.

Mom and Dad went out.

Sing this song.

Play that tune.

Move the box

The last game was fun.

Sit in the chair.

Close the door, please.

Go to the pool.

Run home for lunch.

Are you sad?

We can go home now.

When will you leave.

Turn this way.

Go this way to school.

AWARENESS OF WHOLE WORDS AS UNITS OF SOUND (ADVANCED)

Activity 2

Aim: To consolidate the children's recognition of words as separate units of sound.

Learning Outcome: CHILDREN WILL RESPOND ACCURATELY TO THREE, FOUR OR FIVE WORD STRINGS (INVOLVING ONE OR TWO SYLLABLES), BY MOVING CUBES (OR COUNTERS) INTO THREE, FOUR OR FIVE BOXES.

Materials:
Fig. 1 — A five-square grid per child
Fig. 3 — List of sentences

Method:
1. Give out the cubes (counters) and a five-square grid to each child.

2. Explain, as before, that the children move a cube (counter) into a box for each word of the sentence.

3. Practice and check, as before, with item one from Fig. 3.

4. Continue with the remaining sentences.

AWARENESS OF WHOLE WORDS AS UNITS OF SOUND (ADVANCED)

Fig. 3

LIST OF SENTENCES FOR ACTIVITY 2

He was running home early.

Are you happy?

Come swimming with me today.

Tell me a funny story.

What will happen next?

He played soccer after school.

Come home for supper.

Did you call Mother?

He is laughing.

The dog jumped the fence.

The girl shouted very loudly.

The flowers are growing.

It is scary.

He needed more help.

Hopscotch is fun.

It is a happy day.

She pulled the heavy cart.

The baby cried.

They are running.

It costs lots of money.

AWARENESS OF WHOLE WORDS AS UNITS OF SOUND (ADVANCED)

ACTIVITY 3

AIM:
To revise the concept of beginning, middle, and end, as applied to words in sentence.

LEARNING OUTCOME:

CHILDREN WILL MOVE A CUBE (COUNTER) TO THE BEGINNING, MIDDLE, OR END OF A PICTURE GRID.

MATERIALS:
Fig. 4 — Picture grid
Fig. 5 — List of sentences

METHOD:

1. Say, *"I will say a sentence. Listen carefully. Then, I will say one of the words."*
"Look at your picture grid. The head shows where the beginning is." Point to the beginning box.
"The middle of the cat shows where the middle is." Point to the middle box.
"The tail of the cat shows where the end is." Point to the end box.

2. Say, *"Listen to this sentence. Tell me the word at the beginning. Move the cube to the right place."*
"Flowers are blue"
"Flowers"

3. Check that the children all moved their cubes to the beginning box.

4. Use the same format for the other sentences, checking each time that the children move their cubes correctly.

Fig. 4

AWARENESS OF WHOLE WORDS
AS UNITS OF SOUND (ADVANCED)

AWARENESS OF WHOLE WORDS AS UNITS OF SOUND (ADVANCED)

Fig. 5

LIST OF SENTENCES FOR ACTIVITY 3

Flowers are blue.	(flowers)
Trees are green.	(green)
Birds fly fast.	(fly)
Children sing loudly.	(sing)
How are you?	(how)
We are ready.	(ready)
Sing this song.	(sing)
Are you happy?	(are)
Mom is here.	(is)
Play that tune.	(tune)
Move the box.	(move)
Are you sad?	(you)
Time to play.	(play)
Turn this way.	(turn)
Get ready quickly.	(ready)
Your turn now.	(your)
Can you ski?	(ski)
Come home, James.	(James)
Light those candles.	(light)
Drive his car.	(his)

AWARENESS OF WHOLE WORDS AS UNITS OF SOUND (ADVANCED)

ACTIVITY 4

AIM: To consolidate children's recognition of words as separate units of sound.

LEARNING OUTCOME:

> CHILDREN WILL SHOW WITH THEIR FINGERS THE NUMBER OF WORDS THEY HEAR WHEN THEIR NEIGHBOUR WHISPERS ONE, TWO OR THREE WORDS TO THEM. CHILDREN WILL ALSO CHECK OTHER CHILDREN.

MATERIALS: Fig. 6 — Word List

METHOD:

1. Choose one child in the group to come close to you. Whisper not more than three words from Fig. 6. Say, *"I will whisper some words to _____. Listen carefully. Show me with your finger each time you hear a word"*. Pace the words slowly, so the child easily shows a finger in time with each word. Say whether the child was right or wrong and share with the group.

2. Now whisper another set of words to child '1' (same child), so that child '1' can whisper those words to child '2'. Ask child '1' to check that child '2' held up the right number of fingers.

3. Repeat this game all around the group, so that each has a turn at hearing and showing how many words with their fingers, followed by whispering and checking with the next child along.

4. There are enough items in Fig. 6 to go all round the group twice, using the items with two syllables on the second go.

9

AWARENESS OF WHOLE WORDS AS UNITS OF SOUND (ADVANCED)

Fig. 6

WORD LIST FOR ACTIVITY 4

(A)

1. Come with me.
2. Play this game.
3. Run fast.
4. Dance
5. Shut the door.
6. Brown cow.

(B)

1. Loudly.
2. Come quickly.
3. Rain is falling.
4. Flowers are red.
5. Skipping.
6. Skating.

(C)

1. My stomach hurts badly.
2. Lions roar fiercely.
3. Sisters play.
4. Laughing.
5. Ducks are yellow.
6. Trains go very fast.

AWARENESS OF WHOLE WORDS AS UNITS OF SOUND (ADVANCED)

ACTIVITY 5

AIM: To consolidate children's recognition of words as separate units of sound.

LEARNING OUTCOME:

> CHILDREN WILL PRODUCE THEIR OWN WORD STRINGS OF BETWEEN ONE AND SIX WORDS.

MATERIALS: Fig. 7 — Spinner

METHOD:

1. Say, *"We are all going to have a turn with the spinner. If the spinner stops on one, just think up one word, like 'smile'. If the spinner stops on three, just think up three words, like 'Smile at me'"*.

2. Say, *"Watch me spin the spinner."*
   Adult spins and produces the appropriate word string.

3. Let every child have a turn and repeat as often as desired.

AWARENESS OF WHOLE WORDS
AS UNITS OF SOUND (ADVANCED)

Fig. 7

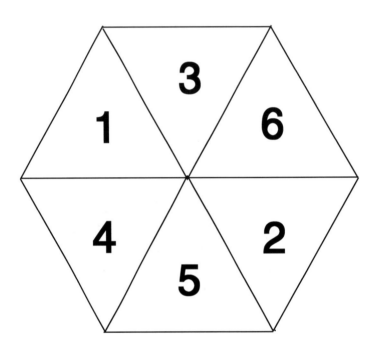

RHYME (ADVANCED)

ACTIVITY 1

AIM:

To practice finding the odd one out from three-word strings (including a rhyming pair) given verbally.

LEARNING OUTCOME:

> CHILDREN WILL SAY THE ODD ONE OUT VERBALLY.

MATERIALS:

Fig. 8 — Word list

METHOD:

1. Say, *"Listen to these three words. Two of them rhyme but one of them doesn't. It is the odd one out. For example, red, bed, green. Which is the old one out?"*

   *"Yes, **green** is the odd one out."*

2. Using the words from Fig. 8, give another example. Encourage the children to raise their hand if they know the answer. Listen to all answers, but repeat the correct answer. Notice any child who is having trouble and provide appropriate support. For example, repeat the words more slowly, saying, *"Listen to these words again...."*.

3. Repeat the words from Fig. 8. Give each child a turn until the list is completed. Repeat as often as necessary.

RHYME (ADVANCED)

Fig. 8

WORD LIST FOR ACTIVITY 1

(A)

1.	red	bed	green
2.	shoe	sock	blue
3.	pen	cow	now
4.	cat	home	sat
5.	luck	not	duck
6.	pie	tie	win

(B)

1.	black	sack	clock
2.	bread	toast	read
3.	green	throne	lean
4.	bring	sung	sing
5.	cheese	please	glass
6.	cake	like	lake

(C)

1.	table	able	rain
2.	ship	tailor	sailor
3.	elf	slip	shelf
4.	mother	brother	sister
5.	plenty	ten	twenty

14

RHYME (ADVANCED)

ACTIVITY 2

AIM:
To practice finding a pair of words that rhyme from three-word strings (including a rhyming pair) given verbally.

LEARNING OUTCOME:

CHILDREN WILL SAY THE RHYMING PAIR VERBALLY.

MATERIALS:
Fig. 9 — Word list

METHOD:
1. Explain that you are going to say three words. Two of them rhyme but one of them doesn't. Ask the children to say which two words rhyme — 'pig', 'wig', 'hand'.

2. Using the words from Fig. 9, give another example. Encourage the children to raise their hand if they know the correct answer. Listen to all the answers but repeat the correct answer.
Again, notice any child who is having trouble and provide appropriate support. For example, repeat the words more slowly.

3. Repeat the words from Fig. 9. Give each child a turn until the list is completed.

RHYME (ADVANCED)

Fig. 9

WORD LIST FOR ACTIVITY 2

(A)

1.	bag	flag	sat
2.	cup	jug	mug
3.	mouse	dog	house
4.	sun	log	run
5.	van	man	bus
6.	boy	tall	wall

(B)

1.	ramp	stamp	hope
2.	sand	sea	land
3.	sky	blue	true
4.	jump	swim	bump
5.	chop	shop	buy
6.	mask	flask	fish

(C)

1.	candy	dandy	sweet
2.	window	flutter	butter
3.	flower	spring	shower
4.	making	shaking	print
5.	rabit	habit	hunter

16

RHYME (ADVANCED)

ACTIVITY 3

AIM:

To elicit a word that rhymes with two other words shown in pictures.

LEARNING OUTCOME:

CHILDREN WILL PRODUCE WORDS WHICH RHYME EACH TIME WITH TWO OTHERS SHOWN IN PICTURES.

MATERIALS:

Figs. 10, 11 and 12 — Pictures of word pairs that rhyme

METHOD:

1. Give out photocopied picture sheets (Figs. 10, 11, and 12) to each child.

2. Say, *"Let's name the pictures on this sheet. Now I will say the picture names. Can you give another word that rhymes with these two?"*

3. Repeat for all items in Figs. 10. 11 and 12.

RHYME (ADVANCED)

Fig. 10

Picture List for Activity 3

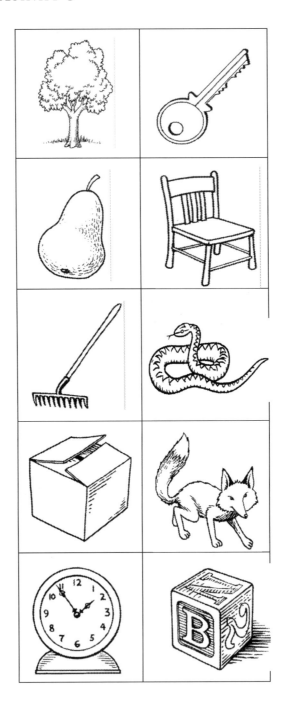

RHYME (ADVANCED)

Fig. 11

Picture List for Activity 3

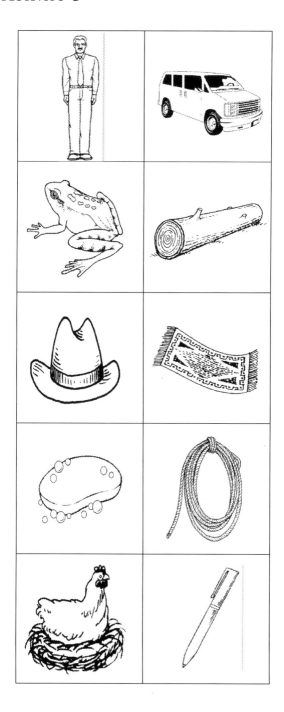

RHYME (ADVANCED

Fig. 12

PICTURE LIST FOR ACTIVITY 3

RHYME (ADVANCED)

ACTIVITY 4

AIM: To elicit up to three words that rhyme with a stimulus picture word.

LEARNING OUTCOME:

> CHILDREN WILL PRODUCE REAL OR NONSENSE WORDS THAT RHYME WITH THEIR OWN PICTURE CARD.

MATERIALS: Fig. 13 — (Needs cutting up. Can be mounted on card and laminated.)
Many small counters in a box.

METHOD:

1. Give each child a card. Say, *"Think of as many words as you can that rhyme with your picture."*
(Nonsense words are accepted.)

2. Let each child take a turn to produce as many rhyming words as possible.

3. Take the cards in, shuffle them, and redistribute. Everyone has another turn.

4. Repeat as above, <u>but</u> this time tell the children, *"You will get a counter for each <u>real</u> word you say that rhymes with your picture."*

    Praise the winner of the most counters each time, and repeat as many times as necessary.

RHYME (ADVANCED)

ACTIVITY 5

AIM: To practice generating real or nonsense rhyming words in a continuous group story.

LEARNING OUTCOME:

CHILDREN WILL CONTRIBUTE NONSENSE OR REAL WORDS THAT RHYME WITH THE STIMULUS LINE.

MATERIALS: Fig. 14 — Stimulus story with blanks to be filled in with nonsense or real words that rhyme.

METHOD:

1. Say, *"Here's a funny story. Listen carefully because there are some clues to help you fill in rhyming words. the rhyming words can be silly words or real words."*

2. Let the children call out their words as they listen. If more than one child suggests a word, let the group agree which one fits the best.

RHYME (ADVANCED)

Fig. 14

Once upon a time .....
Two monkeys lived in the zoo,
One named Fred and one named _____.
Fred played in the hay.
He played all _____.

Until .... one day they visited the rest of the zoo.
What did they see?
Two frogs lived under a stone.
By themselves they loved to _____.
In the morning they jumped and swam.
In the evening they ate bread and _____.

A lazy lion sat under a tree.
He said, "Does anyone look as handsome as ____?"

Gerry Giraffe is very tall
But minuscule mouse is very _____.

Little red hen was in her pen
But the woolly sheep had gone to _____.

ONSET AND RIME (ADVANCED)

ACTIVITY 1

AIM:
To have children analyze a word into onset and rime format verbally.

LEARNING OUTCOME:

CHILDREN WILL BE ABLE TO HEAR A WHOLE WORD AND THEN SAY IT AS AN ONSET AND A RIME.

MATERIALS:
Fig. 15 — Word list
Puppet to share, or individual puppets (e.g. finger puppets)

METHOD:

1. Say, *"I will say a word — **dog**. Listen carefully and make your puppet say it, in a bumpy voice, like this — **d---og**. Let's do the same with fish, **f---ish**.*

   Do you hear that we are always splitting off the first sound and leaving behind the rest. So we always say the word in two parts."

2. Say, *"Now are you ready with your puppets, because I'm going to say some words for each of you in turn."*

   Use the words in Fig. 15. If a child finds it difficult, model how to do it, and let the child practice.

3. Ensure that each child has a turn.

ONSET AND RIME (ADVANCED)

Fig. 15

Word List for Activity 1

old	ring
cake	boat
wing	lock
fix	watch
bike	belt
light	coat
rope	sock
hand	doll
bold	jump
hill	sing
night	most
rock	melt

ONSET AND RIME (ADVANCED)

ACTIVITY 2

AIM: To have children analyze a word into onset and rime format verbally.

LEARNING OUTCOME:

CHILDREN WILL BE ABLE TO NAME A PICTURE, THERE-FORE SAYING A WHOLE WORD THEMSELVES, BEFORE SPLITTING THE WORD INTO ITS ONSET AND RIME PARTS.

MATERIALS: Fig. 16 — Grid
Figs. 17, 18, 19, 20, 21, 22, 23, 24 — Pictures
Unifix® Cubes — 3 per child

METHOD:
1. Give out cubes, and Fig. 16 to each child.

2. Explain to the children that they will use their cubes to show two parts of each word.

3. Say, *"I will show you a picture. Say the name of the picture and then split the name as your puppet did."*

4. Model how to move one cube into the small space while naming the onset, and two cubes into the larger space while naming the rime.

5. Ask the children to try this with all the other pictures.

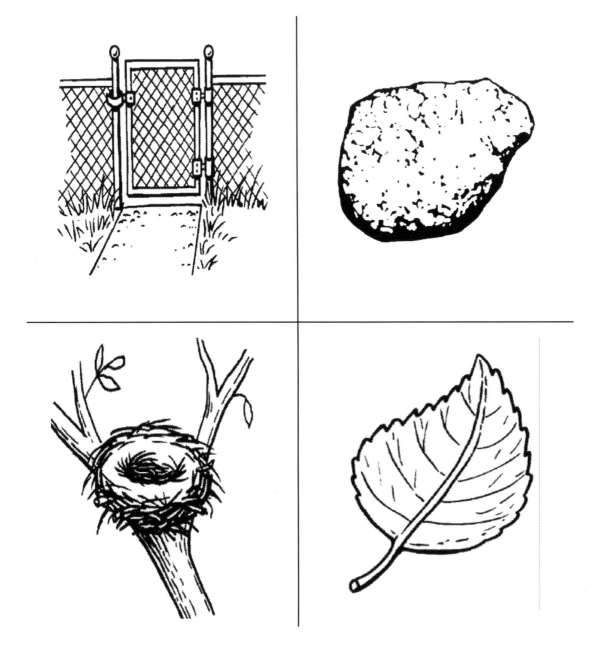

Fig. 19

9

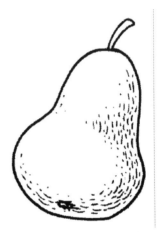

4   5

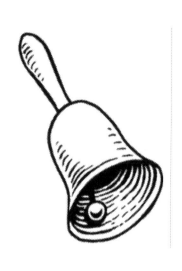

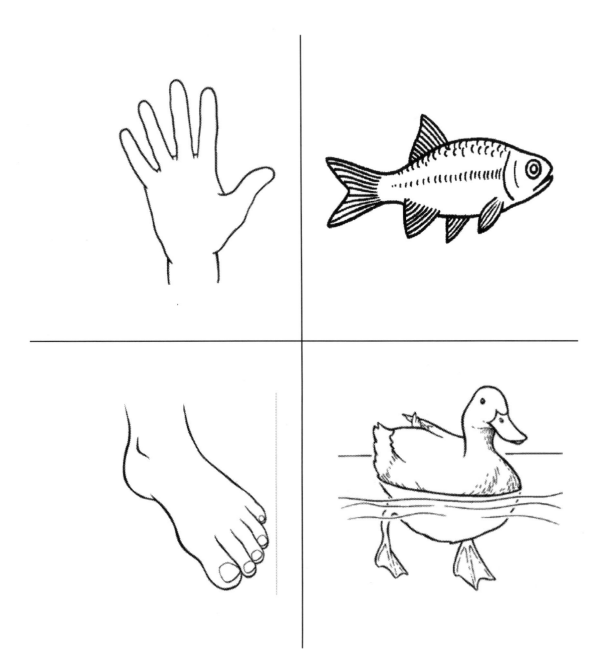

ONSET AND RIME (ADVANCED)

Activity 3

AIM:

To have children synthesize given onset and rimes into whole words.

LEARNING OUTCOME:

> CHILDREN WILL SAY WHOLE WORDS AFTER HEARING WORDS AS ONSET AND RIMES.

MATERIALS:

Puppet
Fig. 25 — Word list

METHOD:

1. Say, *"Listen carefully. Here is Percy, the puppet again, who will say some words in his funny voice. He will say each word in two parts, and I want you to tell me which word he says."*

2. Say, *"Let's practice. Percy says,* **f---our**. *What did Percy say? Yes,* **four**. *Now listen and Percy will say some more parts of words."*

3. Go down the list, giving each child a turn.

ONSET AND RIME (ADVANCED)

Fig. 25

WORD LIST FOR ACTIVITY 3

mouse	ditch
five	sand
wall	nose
road	face
pack	bend
bite	book
hawk	yard
desk	park
paint	dart
door	tooth
cook	mouth
hair	card

ONSET AND RIME (ADVANCED)

ACTIVITY 4

AIM:
To have children synthesize given onset and rimes into whole words.

LEARNING OUTCOME:

> CHILDREN WILL SAY WHOLE WORDS FROM THE PICTURES THEY DRAW IN ONSET AND RIME FORM. CHILDREN WILL ALSO DECIDE WHETHER OR NOT ANOTHER CHILD HAS RESPONDED CORRECTLY.

MATERIALS:
Piece of paper and pencils
Finger puppets for each child

METHOD:

1. Say to the children, *"Think of a word with one beat that you can draw a picture of."*
   (Examples are: leaf, house, dog. They may choose words like these from the previous game.)

2. Say, *"Turn your picture over. Choose a partner. Make your puppet say the name of the picture in a bumpy voice."* Model how to say a name of a picture in onset and rime form (e.g. **b—at**).

3. Allow another child to do the same as before.

4. Let all the children sit in a circle with their picture in front of them.

5. Invite any child to choose another child's picture and make their puppet say the word in a bumpy way. Let them select a child to tell what the word is.

6. Ensure each child has a turn.

DISCRIMINATION — MIDDLE SOUNDS

ACTIVITY 1

AIM:

To introduce children to the concept of middle sounds in words.

LEARNING OUTCOME:

CHILDREN CAN IDENTIFY THE MIDDLE PERSON IN A LINE OF THREE.

MATERIALS:

Spinner to indicate 'beginning', 'middle' and 'end' positions.

METHOD:

1. Three children from the group are chosen to form a short line. Say, "_____ is at the beginning, _____ is at the end. Who is in the middle?" Children answer.

2. Get the children to change positions and say again, "_____ is at the beginning, _____ is at the end. Who is in the middle?"

3. Repeat No. 2, and ask, "Who is in the middle?"

4. Now produce the spinner and show the children how it chooses a child in the group.

5. Now play the game several times, where the child chosen by the spinner takes the middle position in the line.

NOTE:

For those children that may need extra work to build the concept of 'middle', see Fig. 27 — Pictures of hamburger, egg, jelly do-nut, and yoyo. This can be photocopied and used as a stimulus sheet at other times (little and often) by parents and/or other supporting adults.

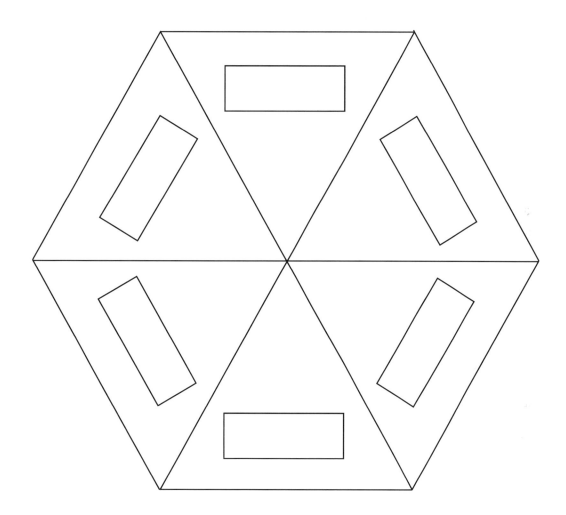

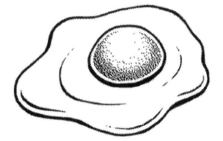

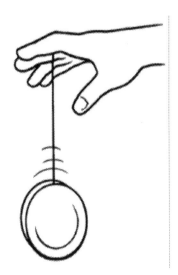

DISCRIMINATION — MIDDLE SOUNDS

ACTIVITY 2

AIM: To introduce children to the concept of middle sounds in words.

LEARNING OUTCOME:

CHILDREN CAN NAME PICTURES WITH THE SAME SOUND IN THE MIDDLE.

MATERIALS: Pictures of pairs of words (Figs. 28 and 29)

1. Say, *"Listen to these two words. The sound in the middle of these words is 'u'."*   (bug, nut)

2. Repeat. *"Listen to these two sounds. What is the sound in the middle of these two words?"*
    Child responds.

3. Repeat, using all the pairs of pictures in Fig. 28 and Fig. 29.
    (Add instructions if the child is not getting it as before).

DISCRIMINATION — MIDDLE SOUNDS

Fig. 28

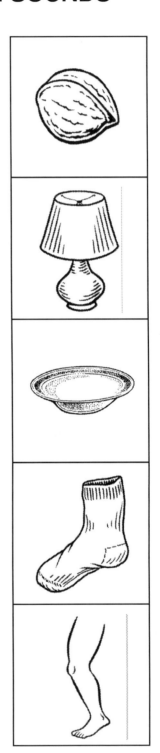

DISCRIMINATION — MIDDLE SOUNDS

Fig. 29

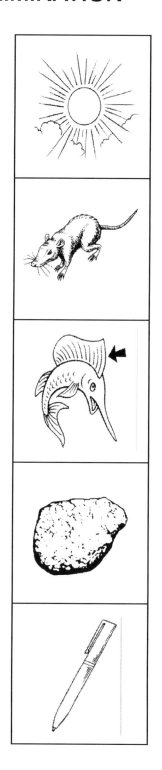
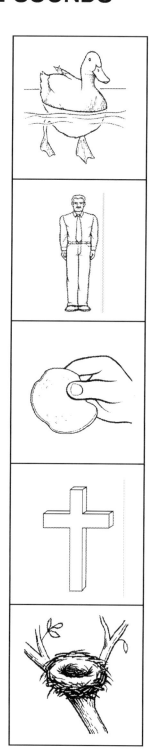

DISCRIMINATION — MIDDLE SOUNDS

ACTIVITY 3

AIM: To introduce children to the concept of middle sounds as words.

LEARNING OUTCOME:

CHILDREN WILL KNOW THE PICTURES THAT HAVE THE SAME SOUND IN THE MIDDLE.

MATERIALS: Fig. 30 — List of words to be read.

METHOD:

1. Say, *"Listen to these two words, 'drag', 'plant'. The sound in the middle of these words is 'a'."*

2. *"Now you try. I will say the words again and you tell me the sound you hear in the middle, 'drag', 'plant'. Yes, the sound is 'a'."*

3. Repeat, using all the pairs of words in Fig. 30.

   Word List for Activity 3, see Fig. 30 following.

WORD LIST

drag	plant
den	left
drip	did
flop	soft
fun	hunt
glad	lap
when	speck
lift	will
stop	not
bump	stuck

DISCRIMINATION — MIDDLE SOUNDS

ACTIVITY 4

AIM:

To let children respond verbally as to whether the names of three picturs have the same sound in the middle.

LEARNING OUTCOME:

> CHILDREN WILL NAME THE SOUND IN THE MIDDLE OF THE THREE WORDS.

MATERIALS:

Fig. 31 — Pictures of sets of three words which each have the same middle sound, one for each child.

METHOD:

1. Say, *"Listen to these three words. The sound in the middle of these words is '**e**'. **Nest**, **bell**, **ten**."*

2. *"Now you try. I will say the words and you tell me the sound that you hear in the middle. **Nest**, **bell**, **ten**."*

3. Give out copies of Fig. 31 to all the children in the group.

4. Name the pictures with the children. Make sure that all children have a turn at naming the pictures.

5. Now ask for the middle sounds in each line of three pictures, e.g. *"Tell me the middle sound in '**net**', '**bed**', '**neck**'."*

6. Continue through all the lines of pictures. Make sure each child has a turn.

DISCRIMINATION — MIDDLE SOUNDS

ACTIVITY 5

AIM:

To let children respond verbally as to whether three words have the same sound in the middle.

LEARNING OUTCOME:

> CHILDREN WILL NAME THE SOUND IN THE MIDDLE OF THE THREE WORDS GIVEN VERBALLY ONLY.
> (I.E. NO PICTURES THIS TIME.)

MATERIALS:

Fig. 32 — Sets of three words the same middle sound

METHOD:

1. Say, *"Listen to these three words. The sound in the middle of these words is 'a'."*

2. *"Now you try. I will say the words and you tell me the sound that you hear in the middle."*

3. Use Fig. 32 to say the next set of words and ask the same questions.

4. Repeat with all the sets of words. Say, *"Tell me the middle sound in _____, _____, _____"*.

Word List for Activity 5, see Fig. 32 following.

DISCRIMINATION— MIDDLE SOUNDS   Fig. 32

Word List

lap	stand	can
chest	step	set
bit	slim	crisp
flock	lost	drop
lump	shut	just
sand	gas	clam
beg	dent	wet
did	rip	fill
jog	pot	romp
rut	dug	such

DISCRIMINATION — MIDDLE SOUNDS

ACTIVITY 6

AIM:
To practice identifying sounds in the middle of words.

LEARNING OUTCOME:

> CHILDREN WILL IDENTIFY WHETHER TWO WORDS HAVE THE SAME SOUND IN THE MIDDLE OR NOT.

MATERIALS:
Fig. 33 — Pairs of words with middle sounds which are alike or different.
Fig. 34 — Spinner
Fig. 35 — Game board - ladder.

METHOD:

1. Say two words. Ask the children, *"Do these two words have the same sound in the middle?"*
   Children answer "Yes" or "No".

2. *"Let's practice with some more words. There are no pictures. Just listen."*

3. *"Now we are going to play a game. When it's your turn, listen to the words. Say '**Yes'** if the middle sounds are the same, or '**No'** if they are different."*

4. Give each child counters and explain that when they have their turn and answer correctly, they can spin the spinner (numbers side) and move the same number of places up the ladder.

5. Use the pairs of words in Fig. 33.

52

DISCRIMINATION— MIDDLE SOUNDS Fig. 33

Word List

1.	tap	sand
2.	west	deck
3.	tan	did
4.	flop	beg
5.	sob	lot
6.	rip	set
7.	bump	shock
8.	can	best
9.	fun	snug
10.	red	kept
11.	skip	pot
12.	chest	set
13.	shut	glad
14.	grin	will
15.	crush	clap
16.	ban	fast
17.	dust	but
18.	hit	mad
19.	drag	lap
20.	fist	fox

Fig. 34

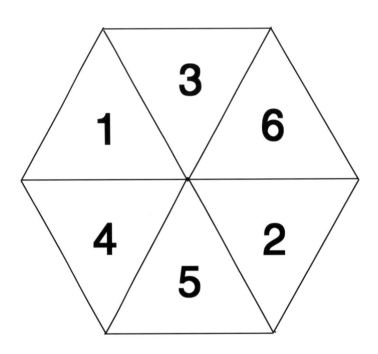

DISCRIMINATION— MIDDLE SOUNDS

Fig. 35

30
29
28
27
26
25
24
23
22
21

20
19
18
17
16
15
14
13
12
11

10
9
8
7
6
5
4
3
2
1

DISCRIMINATION — MIDDLE SOUNDS

ACTIVITY 7

AIM: To identify the one middle sound which is different when three pictures are presented.

LEARNING OUTCOME:

> CHILDREN WILL IDENTIFY WHICH OF THE THREE PICTURES IS THE ODD ONE OUT.

MATERIALS: Fig. 36 — Pictures of sets of three words in which one middle sound is different and two are the same. One set for each child.

METHOD:

1. Give out the pictures.

2. Say. *"Listen to these three words. One of the middle sounds is different from the other two."* Point to each of the pictures in the top line.

3. *"Listen: 'cup', 'man', 'rug'. Can you hear which one sounds different in the middle?"*

   Repeat: **'cup'**, **'man'**, **'rug'**.
   "Yes, 'man' sounds different in the middle.

4. Now, point to the pictures on the next line.
   "Let's say them. Which one sounds different in the middle."

5. Go through each line in the same way.

6. Children can finish by colouring in the pictures of those sounds that are the same.

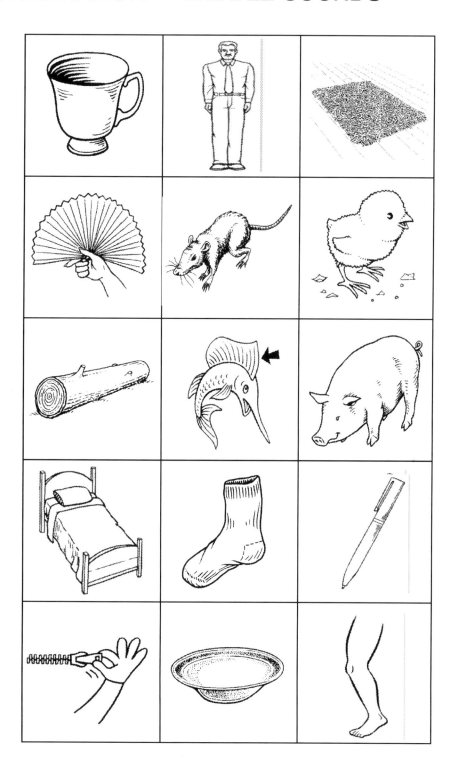

DISCRIMINATION — MIDDLE SOUNDS

Activity 8

AIM: To identify the odd middle sound when three words are given verbally only.

LEARNING OUTCOME:

> CHILDREN WILL IDENTIFY WHICH OF THE THREE WORDS THEY HEAR IS THE ODD ONE.

MATERIALS: Fig. 37 — List of words in sets of three, where one is different from the other two.

METHOD:

1. *"This time there are no pictures. Listen carefully."*
   Say three words (top three on Fig. 37).
   Ask the children, *"Do all these words have the same sound in the middle?"*
   Children answer, *"Yes"* or *"No"*.
   Say, *"No, one word has a different sound in the middle. 'Den' has a different sound in the middle."*

2. *"Let's practice with some more sets of words. There are no pictures, so listen very carefully."*

3. Go through all the sets of words on Fig. 37. Ensure each child has a turn.

   Word List for Activity 8, see Fig. 37 following.

WORD LIST

drag	trap	den
red	bet	trip
gas	stop	lap
can	sad	grin
rip	fill	drop
cut	fun	mist
run	wet	jump
glad	hut	dug
did	tan	will

DISCRIMINATION MIDDLE SOUNDS

ACTIVITY 9

AIM: To identity the picture with a middle sound that is the same as the other two middle sounds.

LEARNING OUTCOME:

CHILDREN WILL CUT AND PASTE PICTURES WITH THE SAME MIDDLE SOUND AS THE OTHER TWO PICTURES.

MATERIALS: Fig. 38 — Pictures of two words in which the middle sound is the same.
Fig. 39 — A list of pictures, one of which will match the blank in Fig. 38
Scissors and paste

METHOD: 1. Give out the pictures with a blank space.

2. Say, "*Listen to the names of these pictures. Find a picture that has the same sound in the middle as* **'cup'**, **'rug'**.

3. "*Yes,* **'sun'** *has the same sound in the middle as* **'cup'** *and* **'rug'**."

4. Repeat, using the other pictures.

60

DISCRIMINATION— MIDDLE SOUNDS

Fig. 38

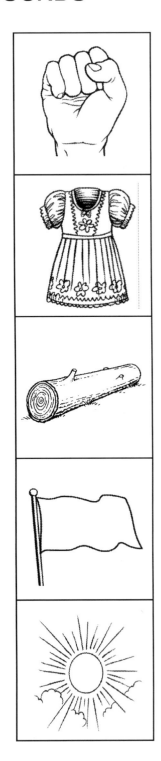

DISCRIMINATION — MIDDLE SOUNDS

ACTIVITY 10

AIM: To identify particular middle sounds in sets of words given verbally.

LEARNING OUTCOME:
> CHILDREN WILL TELL WHICH MIDDLE SOUND THEY HEAR IN GIVEN SETS OF WORDS.

MATERIALS: Fig. 40 — Sets of words which have a common middle sound which the children will name.

METHOD:

1. Say, *"Tell me the sound you hear in the middle of these words"*.

2. Use Fig. 40 to present sets of three words where the sound in the middle is the same. Children will name the sound.

   Word List for Activity 10, see Fig. 40 following.

DISCRIMINATION— MIDDLE SOUNDS

Fig. 40

WORD LIST

jog	soft	long
big	did	bit
left	when	deck
glad	tan	gas
hut	jump	crush
drag	land	clap
west	set	beg
rip	slim	wit
lump	stuck	just
kept	speck	red
ban	strap	fast
flock	pond	stop

DISCRIMINATION— MIDDLE SOUNDS

ACTIVITY 11

AIM:
To produce new words with the same middle sound as the two given.

LEARNING OUTCOME:

> CHILDREN WILL PRODUCE A NEW WORD OF THEIR OWN WITH THE SAME MIDDLE SOUND AS THE TWO WORDS GIVEN.

MATERIALS:
Fig. 41 — List of pairs of words

METHOD:

1. Say, *"Listen to these two words. Both have the same sound in the middle. Think of another word with the same middle sound - e.g.* **'stop'**, **'lost'**.*"*

2. *"Yes,* **'stop'**, **'lost'**, *and* **'cross'** *have the same middle sound."*

3. Repeat with the other pairs of words.

4. Try to ensure that each child has a turn. It may be necessary to support some children to ensure success, with very positive language.

Word List for Activity 11, see Fig. 41 following.

DISCRIMINATION— MIDDLE SOUNDS Fig. 41

WORD LIST

stop	lost
drip	grin
speck	rent
clap	stand
fun	hunt
last	glad
when	left
rip	wish
hot	shock
bump	crush
clam	gas
step	lend
mist	skip

DISCRIMINATION — MIDDLE SOUNDS

ACTIVITY 12

AIM:

To review sets of words in which, 'beginning', 'middle', or 'ending' sounds may be the same.

LEARNING OUTCOME:

CHILDREN WILL IDENTIFY WHETHER THE SOUNDS ARE THE SAME AT THE BEGINNING, MIDDLE, OR END.

MATERIALS:

Fig. 42 — Sets of three words which are mixed. They may have the same beginning, middle or end sounds.

METHOD:

1. Say, "*I am going to say a set of three words. How are they the same?*"

   "*Yes, 'sand', 'set', 'sit' are all the same at the beginning.*"

2. Repeat, using the other sets of three words.

   Word List for Activity 12, see Fig. 42 following.

DISCRIMINATION— MIDDLE SOUNDS

Fig. 42

WORD LIST

Beginning:	sand	set	sit
	jog	jump	jolly
	get	grand	gold
	did	dam	deck
End:	sob	grab	tub
	west	pat	hunt
	grass	sits	dress
	bag	rig	long
Middle:	lump	crust	dug
	fan	mast	glad
	den	egg	set
	lift	rip	grin
Mixed:	grass	sits	dress	*(ending)*
	den	egg	set	*(middle)*
	get	grand	gold	*(beginning)*
	sob	grab	tub	*(ending)*
	lump	crust	dug	*(middle)*
	did	dam	deck	*(beginning)*

ANALYSIS AND SYNTHESIS OF PHONEMES

ACTIVITY 1

AIM: To teach children how to analyze words into phonemes.

LEARNING OUTCOME:

> CHILDREN WILL SAY THE NAME OF A PICTURE AND WILL PRONOUNCE IT AS PHONEMES, WHILE CUTTING IT UP INTO THE CORRECT NUMBER OF PARTS.

MATERIALS:
Fig. 43 — Zoo   (2 phonemes)
Fig. 44 — Dog   (3 phonemes)
Fig. 45 — Frog   (4 phonemes)
Scissors
Percy the Puppet (for adult)

METHOD:

1. Say, *"Do you remember how Percy, the puppet, spoke in a bumpy way? He said, 'd-/--og' for dog. Now he is going to say dog in a different bumpy way. Listen, he is going to say, 'd-/-o-/-g'. What does he mean?"*

2. *"Percy can split words into parts. We are going to practice splitting words like Percy. Here are some pictures. Let's split them by cutting them up."*

3. Give out the pictures. Encourage each child to say the phonemes as they cut the pictures.

4. Encourage the children to name the picture as a whole word before they cut it up, but then they say the broken-up phonemes as their outcome.

   This activity is about analysis (breaking words apart). Synthesis will follow.

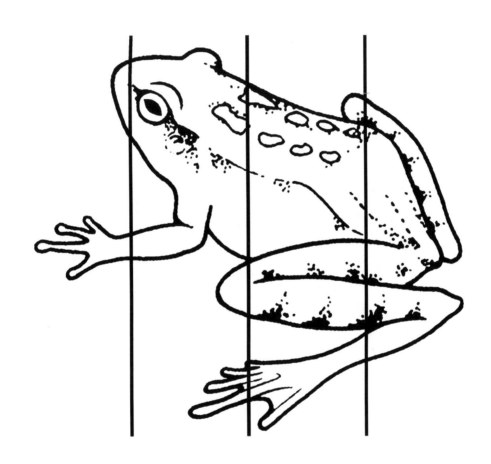

ANALYSIS AND SYNTHESIS OF PHONEMES

ACTIVITY 2

AIM: To teach children how to analyze words into phonemes.

LEARNING OUTCOME:

CHILDREN WILL BE TO ABLE TO HEAR A WHOLE WORD AND THEN SAY IT AS PHONEMES.

MATERIALS: Fig. 46 — 2 phoneme pictures
                        Fig. 47 — 3 phoneme pictures
                        Fig. 48 — 4 phoneme pictures
                        Set of finger puppets (one for each child)
                        Tray of Unifix® cubes in sticks

METHOD: 1. Give out Figs. 46, 47 and 48 to each child.
                           Give out Unifix cube sticks (sticks of 5 or 6).

                        2. Say the name of the picture and listen for the sounds
                           in the word. Use your puppet to say the name of the
                           picture in a bumpy voice. Break off a cube for each
                           sound that your puppet says.
                           (Adult demonstrates this.)

                        3. Children do the same with each picture.

                        4. The adult can ask children randomly to show the rest
                           of the group how they split the cubes.

73

ANALYSIS AND SYNTHESIS OF PHONEMES

LIST OF WORDS THAT ARE PICTURED FOR:

Two Phoneme Words	Three Phoneme Words	Four Phoneme Words
car	man	train
cow	sun	nest
arm	cat	clock
zoo	dog	cats
two	leaf	crab
four	star	plane

ANALYSIS AND SYNTHESIS OF PHONEMES

ACTIVITY 3

AIM:

To teach children how to analyze words into phonemes.

LEARNING OUTCOME:

> CHILDREN WILL LISTEN TO WHOLE WORDS GIVEN VERBALLY, WILL REPEAT WHAT THEY HEAR WITH THEIR PUPPET, AND THEN SHOW THE NUMBER OF SOUNDS WITH CUBES.

MATERIALS:

Fig. 49 — Word list
Finger puppets
Sticks of cubes

METHOD:

1. Say, *"Remember when your puppet said **dog** in a bumpy way, it sounded like **d / o / g**."*
   "Show me with your cubes how many sounds you hear."

2. *"Well done. Let's try another."*
   *"**Key**. Make your puppet say **key** in a bumpy way. Show me with your cubes the number of sounds you hear."*

3. Adult repeats using the words in Fig. 49. Ensure each child has several turns.

ANALYSIS AND SYNTHESIS OF PHONEMES   Fig. 49

WORD LIST

key	(2)		shy	(2)
dig	(3)		cave	(3)
tie	(2)		ray	(2)
house	(3)		tea	(2)
day	(2)		jeep	(3)
rash	(3)		full	(3)
toe	(2)		nose	(3)
save	(3)		row	(2)
hay	(2)		bow	(2)
room	(3)		laugh	(3)

WORD LIST

car	(2)	sun	(3)
man	(3)	star	(3)
train	(4)	cat	(3)
cow	(2)	dog	(3)
arm	(2)	nest	(4)
zoo	(2)	clock	(4)
two	(2)	cats	(4)
four	(2)	crab	(4)
leaf	(3)	plane	(4)

ANALYSIS AND SYNTHESIS OF PHONEMES

ACTIVITY 4

AIM:

To teach children how to analyze words into phonemes.

LEARNING OUTCOME:

> CHILDREN WILL BE ABLE TO HEAR A WHOLE WORD AND SAY IT AS PHONEMES.

MATERIALS:

Fig. 50 — List of small, confusable, but high-frequency words which have only two phonemes.
Finger puppets
Cubes

METHOD:

1. Say, *"There are some very common, very small words which you will be able to make your puppet say in a bumpy way."*

2. *"Listen to this word:* **on**.*"*
   "Now make your puppet say it in a bumpy way."
   "Good."

3. *"This time, listen to another of those little words:* **at**.*"*
   "Now, make the puppet say **at**, *and also show the number of sounds with cubes."*

4. Go through all the words on Fig. 50.
   Alternate use of the cubes with speech only.

ANALYSIS AND SYNTHESIS OF PHONEMES   Fig. 50

WORD LIST

if	of
on	us
at	do
up	in
is	it
an	me
to	go

ANALYSIS AND SYNTHESIS OF PHONEMES

ACTIVITY 5

AIM: To teach children how to analyze words into phonemes.

LEARNING OUTCOME:
CHILDREN WILL BE ABLE TO HEAR A WHOLE NON-WORD (WORD WITHOUT MEANING) AND SAY IT AS PHONEMES.

MATERIALS:
Fig. 51 — List of non-words
Finger puppets
Cubes

METHOD:
1. Say, *"Here are some words that are not real words. They have no meaning. Your puppets can say these words in a bumpy way, too. Let's try some. Make your puppets say the words after me."*

2. Repeat Step 1, using the words from Fig. 51. Ensure each child has one or more turns.

ANALYSIS AND SYNTHESIS OF PHONEMES   Fig. 51

WORD LIST

dit	leck
hing	leng
sond	tunk
wob	jub
sib	vist
pog	vock

ANALYSIS AND SYNTHESIS OF PHONEMES

ACTIVITY 6

AIM:
To teach children the concept of blending individual phonemes into words.

LEARNING OUTCOME:

CHILDREN WILL SHOW BY "MOVING AND SAYING" THAT THEY CAN BLEND TWO, THREE AND FOUR PHONEME WORDS.

MATERIALS:
Fig. 52 — Picture sheet: pie, boy, bee, tie (2)
Fig. 53 — Picture sheet: cup, gate, pig, door (3)
Fig. 54 — Picture sheet: table, lamp, frog, snake (4)

METHOD:

1. Say, *"When Percy, the puppet, says a word, we will move our cubes into the boxes to show the number of bumpy sounds in the word. Let's do the first one together. Percy says, **p—ie**."*

   Adult shows how to move the cubes to match the phonemes in "pie".

Pictures for Activity 6

PICTURES FOR ACTIVITY 6

PICTURES FOR ACTIVITY 6

ANALYSIS AND SYNTHESIS OF PHONEMES

ACTIVITY 7

AIM:
To teach children the concept of blending individual phonemes into words.

LEARNING OUTCOME:

CHILDREN WILL HEAR TWO, THREE AND FOUR PHONEMES SEPARATELY AND THEN WILL BLEND THEM INTO WHOLE WORDS.

MATERIALS:
Fig. 55 — Word list
Fig. 56 — Blank grid to be a model
Puppet
Cubes (split up in tray)
Paper and pencils

METHOD:

1. Give out paper and pencils. Have the cubes available (middle of table).

2. Say, *"Percy, the puppet, will say a word in a bumpy way. Listen carefully. Take a cube for each sound that you hear. Draw a box for each cube."*
Show the children Fig. 56 (top part).

3. *"Now, can you say the whole word that Percy really meant."*

4. Now give all the children turns, saying the whole word and putting the cubes together to show how the sounds come together.

5. At the end of the word list, let the children do a connected grid of their own. (See Fig. 56.)

ANALYSIS AND SYNTHESIS OF PHONEMES

Fig. 55

WORD LIST

four	(2)	clap	(4)
gum	(3)	tea	(2)
plug	(4)	Mom	(3)
arm	(2)	Dad	(3)
slip	(4)	spot	(4)
pat	(3)	stop	(4)
hop	(3)	rap	(3)
car	(2)	trip	(4)
film	(4)	trap	(4)
lot	(3)	rip	(3)

gum

gum

ANALYSIS AND SYNTHESIS OF PHONEMES

ACTIVITY 8

AIM:
To teach children the concept of blending individual phonemes.

LEARNING OUTCOME:

> CHILDREN WILL SAY THE WORDS IN THE PICTURES IN A BUMPY WAY WITH THEIR OWN FINGER PUPPETS, IN TURN AS LEADERS. THEY WILL CHECK THAT THE OTHERS HAVE PUT THE RIGHT NUMBER OF CUBES TOGETHER.

MATERIALS:
Figs. 52, 53 54 as in Activity 6
Finger puppets
Unifix® cubes

METHOD:

1. Give out the pictures to each child.

2. Say, *"Each person will make their puppet speak in a bumpy way."*
   Model how to do this.

3. Now let one child at a time make their puppet say a word. Everyone else in the group puts their cubes together to show the number of sounds they heard.

4. Say to the child leading, *"Choose a person to say the whole word. Did they say it correctly?"*

5. Repeat Step 3 until each child has had one or more turns and all the pictures have been used.

ANALYSIS AND SYNTHESIS OF PHONEMES

ACTIVITY 9

AIM:
To teach children the concept of blending individual phonemes.

LEARNING OUTCOME:

> CHILDREN WILL BE ABLE TO BUILD COMMON TWO-PHONEME WORDS WHEN THE WORDS ARE SAID SPLIT-UP BUT IN A PHRASE.

MATERIALS:
Fig. 57 — Word list
Percy the puppet

METHOD:

1. Say, *"Listen to Percy. He will say one bumpy word in a phrase. It is only a little word but a very common one. Can you tell what it is?"*

2. Say the following phrases/sentences from Fig. 57. Ensure each child has a turn at saying the two-phoneme word.

3. Repeat, using all the words.

WORD LIST

O—n the table	(on)
G—o away	(go)
We are a—t school	(at)
Run t—o the door	(to)
Walk u—p the hill	(up)
Mom i—s home	(is)
A—n apple a day	(an)
Walk i—f clear	(if)
Come i—n here	(in)
I—t was late	(it)
Queen o—f Hearts	(of)
Give u—s food	(us)
D—o come over	(do)
Stay with m—e	(me)

ANALYSIS AND SYNTHESIS OF PHONEMES

ACTIVITY 10

AIM: To teach children the concept of blending individual phonemes.

LEARNING OUTCOME:

> CHILDREN WILL BE ABLE TO HEAR THE PHONEMES IN NONSENSE WORDS AND THEN SAY THE WHOLE NONSENSE PHRASE.

MATERIALS: Figs. 51 — List of non-words
Finger puppets

METHOD:

1. Say, *"These words are not real words. They have no meaning. Percy will say these words in a bumpy way, and your puppet will say the word joined together"*

2. *"Let's try some. Percy is going to say **d-i-t**. What did Percy say? Make your puppet say what Percy said."* *"Good."*

3. Repeat with all the words on Fig. 51. Ensure each child has one or more turns.

LINKAGE

ACTIVITY 1

AIM:

To let the children trace and say the sounds of a group of letters (t g c k q v w o u i)

LEARNING OUTCOME:

> CHILDREN WILL SPONTANEOUSLY FIND, TRACE, AND SAY THE SOUNDS OF A GROUP OF LETTERS.

MATERIALS:

Ten Plastic letters (t g c k q v w o u i)
Fig. 58 — Rainbow chart
Sand tray

METHOD:

1. Place letter i on Fig. 58. Point to letter on the rainbow and say, *"This letter says i. You say i."* Child repeats sound. *"Watch me trace the shape of the letter starting here. It's i. You do that."* Child copies.

2. Get the sand tray. *"Now I'll write it in the sand—i. You do that, too."* Child copies and says, *"i"*, using sand tray. *"Well done. Now let's get the letter from the rainbow and trace it again."*

3. Repeat steps 1 and 2 for each of the other letters in this group (t g c k q u w o u i).

4. Positive prompts are vital.

Fig. 58

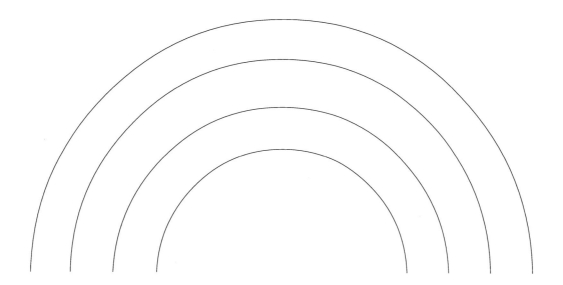

LINKAGE

ACTIVITY 2

AIM:
To let the children trace and say the sounds of a group of letters (**p m j l f r x a i**)

LEARNING OUTCOME:

> CHILDREN WILL SPONTANEOUSLY FIND, TRACE, AND SAY THE SOUNDS OF A GROUP OF LETTERS.

MATERIALS:
Nine Plastic letters (**p m j l f r x a i**)
Fig. 58 — Rainbow chart
Sand tray

METHOD:
1. Place letter **a** on Fig. 58. Point to letter on the rainbow and say, *"This letter says* **a**. *You say* **a**.*"* Child repeats sound. *"Watch me trace the shape of the letter starting here. It's* a. *You do that."* Child copies.

2. Get the sand tray. *"Now I'll write it in the sand—* **a**. *You do that, too."* Child copies and says, *"a"*, using the sand tray. *"Well done. Now let's get the letter from the rainbow and trace it again."*

3. Repeat steps 1 and 2 for each of the other letters in this group (**p m j l f r x a i**).

4. Positive prompts are vital.

LINKAGE

ACTIVITY 3

AIM: To let the children trace and say the sounds of a group of letters (**d n s b y z h o e**)

LEARNING OUTCOME:

CHILDREN WILL SPONTANEOUSLY FIND, TRACE, AND SAY THE SOUNDS OF A GROUP OF LETTERS.

MATERIALS: Nine Plastic letters (**d n s b y z h o e**)
Fig. 58 — Rainbow chart
Sand tray

METHOD: 1. Place letter **i** on Fig. 58. Point to letter on the rainbow and say, *"This letter says* **e**. *You say* **e**.*"*
Child repeats sound. *"Watch me trace the shape of the letter starting here. It's* **e**. *You do that."*
Child copies.

2. Get the sand tray. *"Now I'll write it in the sand—***e**. *You do that, too."* Child copies and says, *"***e***"*, using sand tray. *"Well done. Now let's get the letter from the rainbow and trace it again."*

3. Repeat steps 1 and 2 for each of the other letters in this group (**d n s b y z h o e**).

4. Positive prompts are vital.

99

LINKAGE

Activity 4

Aim: To work further on the relationship between letters and words and to include letter writing

Learning Outcome:

> Children will see and say letter symbols within whole meaningful three-letter words and will print as they say.

Materials:
Fig. 59 — Slide chart
Fig. 60 — Letter shapes sheet, one copy per child
Plastic letters (**d n s b y z h e**)
Pencils

Method:

1. Use Fig. 59 and letters. Choose the plastic letter **e** and have the consonants ready. On Fig. 59 show how **d** can slide down into "**en**", and how **n** can slide down into "**et**", etc.

2. Give out a copy of Fig. 60 and a pencil to each child. Model the first item for the children. Say, *"Look at the letter* **d**. *Say* **d**. *Now look at the next box. With your pencil, trace* **d**, *starting at the big dot."* Check each individual child.

Let children complete sheet.

Fig. 59

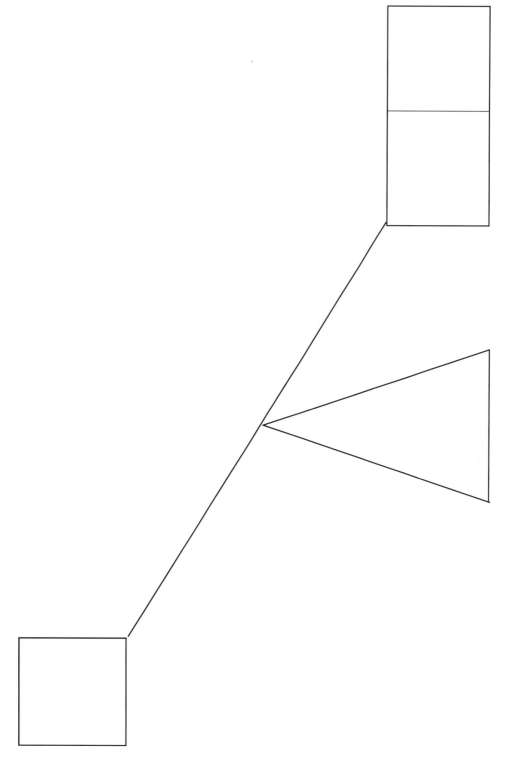

d	d	__	__ en	den
n	n̈	__	__ et	net
s	s·	__	__ ee	see
b	b̈	__	__ ed	bed
y	ÿ	__	__ es	yes
z	·z	__	__ en	zen
h	ḧ	__	__ en	hen

LINKAGE

Activity 5

Aim:

To work further on the relationship between letters and words and to include letter writing

Learning Outcome:

> Children will see and say letter symbols within whole meaningful three-letter words and will print as they say.

Materials:

Fig. 59 — Slide chart
Fig. 61 — Letter shapes sheet, one copy per child
Plastic letters (d n s b y z h o)
Pencils

Method:

1. Use Fig. 59 and letters. Choose the plastic letter **o** and have the consonants ready. On Fig. 59 show how **d** can slide down into "**ot**", and how **n** can slide down into "**od**", etc.

2. Give out a copy of Fig. 61 and a pencil to each child. Model the first item for the children. Say, *"Look at the letter* **d**. *Say* **d**. *Now look at the next box. With your pencil, trace* **d**, *starting at the big dot."* Check each individual child.

   Let children complete sheet.

d	ḋ	__ __ ot	dot
n	n̈	__ __ od	nod
s	s˙	__ __ ob	sob
b	b̈	__ __ oy	boy
y	ÿ	__ __ on	yon
z	z̈	__ __ oo	zoo
h	ḧ	__ __ ot	hot

LINKAGE

Activity 6

AIM: To work further on the relationship between letters and words and to include letter writing

LEARNING OUTCOME:

> CHILDREN WILL SEE AND SAY LETTER SYMBOLS WITHIN WHOLE MEANINGFUL THREE-LETTER WORDS AND WILL PRINT AS THEY SAY.

MATERIALS: Fig. 59 — Slide chart
Fig. 62 — Letter shapes sheet, one copy per child
Plastic letters (t c q v w g k o)
Pencils

METHOD:

1. Use Fig. 59 and letters. Choose the plastic letter **o** and have the consonants ready. On Fig. 59 show how **t** can slide down into "**og**", and how **c** can slide down into "**ow**", etc.

2. Give out a copy of Fig. 62 and a pencil to each child. Model the first item for the children. Say, *"Look at the letter* **t**. *Say* **t**. *Now look at the next box. With your pencil, trace* **t**, *starting at the big dot."* Check each individual child.

   Let children complete sheet.

105

Fig. 62

t	ẗ	__	__ og	tog
c	c	__	__ ow	cow
q	q	__	__ uo	quo
v	v̈	__	__ ow	vow
w	ẅ	__	__ ow	wow
g	g	__	__ ot	got
k	k̈	__	roc__	rock

LINKAGE

ACTIVITY 7

AIM:

To work further on the relationship between letters and words and to include letter writing

LEARNING OUTCOME:

> CHILDREN WILL SEE AND SAY LETTER SYMBOLS WITHIN WHOLE MEANINGFUL THREE-LETTER WORDS AND WILL PRINT AS THEY SAY.

MATERIALS:

Fig. 59 — Slide chart
Fig. 63 — Letter shapes sheet, one copy per child
Plastic letters (t g c q v w k i u)
Pencils

METHOD:

1. Use Fig. 59 and letters. Choose the plastic letter **u** and have the consonants ready. On Fig. 59 show how **t** can slide down into "**ug**", and how **g** can slide down into "**ut**", etc.

2. Give out a copy of Fig. 63 and a pencil to each child. Model the first item for the children. Say, *"Look at the letter* t. *Say* t. *Now look at the next box. With your pencil, trace* t, *starting at the big dot."* Check each individual child.

   Let children complete sheet.

Fig. 63

t	ẗ	__	__ ug	tug
g	g̈	__	__ ut	gut
c	c̈	__	__ ut	cut
q	q̈	__	__ uit	quit
v	v̈	__	__ im	vim
w	ẅ	__	__ ig	wig
k	k̈	__	tuc __	tuck

LINKAGE

Activity 8

AIM: To work further on the relationship between letters and words and to include letter writing

LEARNING OUTCOME:

> CHILDREN WILL SEE AND SAY LETTER SYMBOLS WITHIN WHOLE MEANINGFUL THREE-LETTER WORDS AND WILL PRINT AS THEY SAY.

MATERIALS:
Fig. 59 — Slide chart
Fig. 64 — Letter shapes sheet, one copy per child
Plastic letters (p m j l f r x a)
Pencils

METHOD:

1. Use Fig. 59 and letters. Choose the plastic letter **e** and have the consonants ready. On Fig. 59 show how **p** can slide down into "**al**", and how **m** can slide down into "**ap**", etc.

2. Give out a copy of Fig. 64 and a pencil to each child. Model the first item for the children. Say, *"Look at the letter* **p**. *Say* **p**. *Now look at the next box. With your pencil, trace* **p**, *starting at the big dot."* Check each individual child.

   Let children complete sheet.

Fig. 64

p	p̈	__	__ al	pal
m	m̈	__	__ ap	map
j	j̈	__	__ am	jam
l	ï	__	__ ap	lap
f	f̈	__	__ ax	fax
r	r̈	__	__ ap	rap
x	ẍ	__	ta __	tax

LINKAGE

ACTIVITY 9

AIM:
To work further on the relationship between letters and words and to include letter writing

LEARNING OUTCOME:

CHILDREN WILL SEE AND SAY LETTER SYMBOLS WITHIN WHOLE MEANINGFUL THREE-LETTER WORDS AND WILL PRINT AS THEY SAY.

MATERIALS:
Fig. 59 — Slide chart
Fig. 65 — Letter shapes sheet, one copy per child
Plastic letters (p j m l f r x i)
Pencils

METHOD:
1. Use Fig. 59 and letters. Choose the plastic letter **e** and have the consonants ready. On Fig. 59 show how **p** can slide down into "**ill**", and how **j** can slide down into "**ib**", etc.

2. Give out a copy of Fig.65 and a pencil to each child. Model the first item for the children. Say, *"Look at the letter* **p**. *Say* **p**. *Now look at the next box. With your pencil, trace* **p**, *starting at the big dot."* Check each individual child.

Let children complete sheet.

Fig. 65

p	p̈	__	__ ill	pill
j	j̈	__	__ ib	jib
m	m̈	__	i __ p	imp
l	ï	__	__ ip	lip
f	f̈	__	__ ix	fix
r	r̈	__	__ im	rim
x	ẍ	__	mi __	mix

INTEGRATION OF SOUNDS

AIM:
To read two or three sounds separately, and then blend them into words.

LEARNING OUTCOME:
CHILDREN WILL BE ABLE TO READ WORDS WITH TWO OR THREE SOUNDS IN THEM.

MATERIALS:
Fig. 66 — List of words that consist of two or three sounds
Plastic letters

METHOD:
1. Give each child a copy of Fig. 66. Review the letter sounds in the box (Fig. 66) using the plastic letters.

2. Say, *"Listen to the slow way of saying these sounds — **a / m**. Now listen to the fast way of saying the sounds — **am**. Listen again."* (Repeat step 2).

3. *"Let's try two more sounds. Let's all say it slowly — **a / l**. Now let's all say it fast — **al**."*

4. *"The next word has three sounds. Let's say it slowly... Now let's say it fast..."*

5. Repeat using the other words.

6. Give each child a turn saying all the words slowly and fast, whilst the others follow with their own sheet.

a l p m

a / m

| am |

a / l

| al |

p / a / m

| pam |

m / a / p

| map |

p / a / l

| pal |

l / a / p

| lap |

---

am   al   pam

map   pal   lap

---

a b h t

a / t   h / a   h / a / t

| at | | ha | | hat |

b / a / t   t / a / b   t / a / t

| bat | | tab | | tat |

┌─────────────────────────────────────┐
│   at   ha   hat   │
│   │
│   bat   tab   tat   │
└─────────────────────────────────────┘

INTEGRATION OF SOUNDS

Fig. 68

a d s g

a / s	s /a / d	d / a / d
as	sad	dad
g / a / s	s / a / g	g / a / d
gas	sag	gad

as	sad	dad
gas	sag	gad

Fig. 69

a c f n j k z v

a / n

an

f / a / n

fan

j / a / ck

jack

c / a / n

can

v / a / n

van

j / a / zz

jazz

an   fan   jack

can   van   jazz

i l p m

i / ll

| ill |

p / i / ll

| pill |

m / i / ll

| mill |

l / i / p

| lip |

P / i / m

| Pim |

l / i / mb

| limb |

ill   pill   mill

lip   Pim   limb

INTEGRATION OF SOUNDS

Fig. 71

i d s g

i / s	S / i / d	d / i / g
is	Sid	dig
d / i / d	s / i / s	g / i / d
did	sis	gid

is	Sid	dig
did	sis	gid

Fig. 72

i b h t

i / t

it

b / i / t

bit

h / i / t

hit

t / i / b

tib

h / i / b

hib

b / i / b

bib

it	bit	hit
tib	hib	bib

i c f n j k z v w

i / f

| if |

f / i / n

| fin |

f / i / zz

| fizz |

k / i / n

| kin |

j / i / ff

| jiff |

w / i / n

| win |

```
if          fin          fizz

kin         jiff         win
```

Fig. 74

o d s g h

d / o / g

| dog |

s / o / g

| sog |

h / o / g

| hog |

G / o / d

| God |

h / o / d

| hod |

s / o / d

| sod |

| dog | sog | hog |
| God | hod | sod |

o r t n w x

o / x   n / o / t   w / o / n

ox   not   won

t / o / n   t / o / t   r / o / t

ton   tot   rot

ox	not	won
ton	tot	rot

o p l m t

m / o / p   p / o / p   t / o / p

| mop | pop | top |

p / o / t   l / o / t   T / o / m

| pot | lot | Tom |

mop   pop   top

pot   lot   Tom

o f c j v b n

o / f

of

j / o / b

job

B / o / b

Bob

f / o / b

fob

c / o / b

cob

o / n

on

of   job   Bob

fob   cob   on

e l p m t

e / l / m   p / e / p   m / e / t

| elm | | pep | | met |

l / e / t   p / e / t   t / e / ll

| let | | pet | | tell |

elm   pep   met

pet   let   tell

e m n b t

b / e / n   m / e / n   b / e / t

| ben | | men | | bet |

n / e / t   m / e / t   t / e / n

| net | | met | | ten |

ben   men   bet

net   met   ten

Fig. 80

e g m l f s

s / e / t

| set |

e / l / f

| elf |

m / e / ss

| mess |

b / e / g

| beg |

e / b / b

| ebb |

e / g / g

| egg |

set　　elf　　mess

beg　　ebb　　egg

e f w s l d

f / e / ll

| fell |

s / e / ll

| sell |

w / e / ll

| well |

l / e / ss

| less |

d / e / ll

| dell |

f / e / d

| fed |

fell   sell   well

less   dell   fed

u l p m t

u / p   p / u / t   p / u / ll

up		put		pull

t / u / m   m / u / ll   t / u / t

tum		mull		tut

up   put   pull

tum   mull   tut

u d s g h

s / u / d

sud

h / u / m

hum

d / u / g

dug

h / u / g

hug

g / u / m

gum

m / u / g

mug

sud   hum   dug

hug   gum   mug

INTEGRATION OF SOUNDS

Fig. 84

u b r c n f

r / u/ b	b / u / n	c / u / b
rub	bun	cub
f / u/ n	f / u / r	r / u / n
fun	fur	run

rub	bun	cub
fun	fur	run

u g l b t

l / u / g	b / u / m	t / u / g
lug	bum	tug

b / u / t	g / u / ll	b / u / ll
but	gull	bull

lug   bum   tug

but   gull   bull

PLAYS

AIM: To help children integrate vowel recognition with skills previously taught.

To achieve fluent word and sentence reading through practice and repetition.

LEARNING OUTCOME:

CHILDREN WILL READ THE PLAYS FLUENTLY AS THEY BUILD AUTOMATICITY OF WORD RECOGNITION.

MATERIALS: Copies of plays for each child
Tape recorder and blank audio tapes
Folder for copies of plays for each child

METHOD:

1. Give a copy of the play for the day to each child.

2. Describe the setting of the play.

3. *"Listen carefully and point to the words as I say them. I will be both characters. I will be* (name) *, and then I will be* (name) *.*

4. Now choose two children to read the parts of (name) and (name).

134

5. Say, *"I will help you with hard words"*.
   (Children should not puzzle over words in thse plays.)

6. Let the two readers read the play while all the other children track the words. Be ready to supply any word that the readers are unable to say.

7. Let the other pairs of children read the same play in the same way.

8. Tape record one pair of children reading the play. (Each pair of children can have their turn with each new play). End of session.

9. Before sarting each new play, review the tape made the day before.

10. Add the copies of each new play to each child's folder.

Stories/Plays

Short Vowels

1.	Dinasaur	'a'	12 words
2.	Circus	'e'	14 words
3.	Window Shopping	'i'	12 words
4.	The Ostrich and the Crocodile	'o'	12 words
5.	School Bus	'u'	12 words
6.	Trip to Disneyland	'y'	12 words

Long Vowels

1.	Earthquake	ae	12 words
2.	Train Trip	ai	12 words
3.	Dreams	ea	17 words
4.	Make Believe	ee	12 words
5.	Valentine	ie	10 words
6.	Telephone Talk	oe	14 words
7.	Two cool cats	oo	14 words
8.	Computer	ue	12 words

The Dinosaur

fan

had

mad

ran

van

am

back

dragon

a

man

land

can

The Dinosaur

Pat and Andy are sitting at home looking out of the window at the park.

Pat: I can see a dinosaur.

Andy: A dinosaur! A ... a ... a dino — saur!

Pat: I can really see a dinosaur. I am not mad!

Andy: Where is it?

Pat: It just ran by. It had a fan on its back.

Andy: Was it a man, or a big van?

Pat: No! I saw a dinosaur. Like a dragon, but it was a dinosaur.

Andy: Is the park now a dinosaur land? Let's go to see.

e

Circus

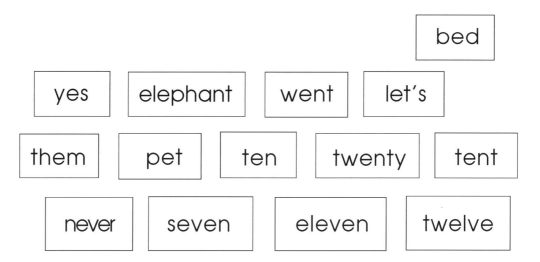

Ted and Erin went to the circus.

Ted: Look at the elephants coming into the tent.

Erin: I can see at least ten elephants.

Ted: There are more. There may be twenty elephants.

Erin: Let's count them.

Ted: Seven   eight   nine   ten   eleven   twelve.

Erin: Yes, now I can see more elephants in the tent.

Ted: I would like an elephant for a pet.

Erin: It would never fit in your bed.

Window Shopping

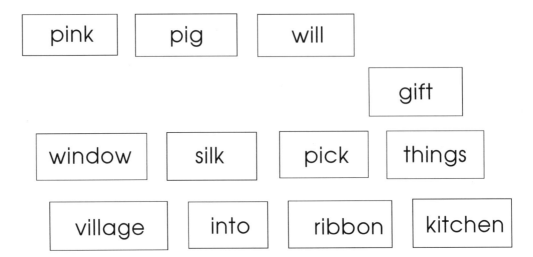

Rick and Simi are in the village.

Rick: Let's go shopping in the village.

Simi: I like the shop windows in the village.

Rick: This window has kitchen things in it.

Simi: Who wants kitchen things? I want that pink pig. I like the one in that window.

Rick: You can pick that pink silk ribbon for your hair.

Simi: Then you can have the pink pig.

Rick: Who wants a pink pig?

Simi: The pink pig with the pink ribbon will make a gift for Jill.

Ostrich and the Crocodile

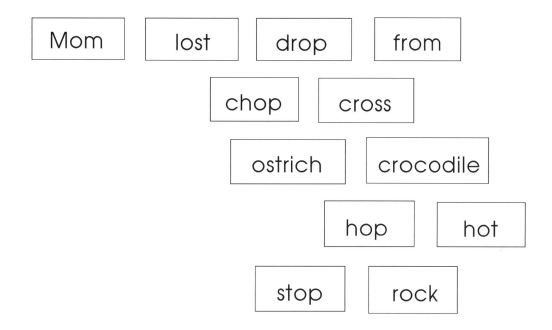

Ostrich sees crocodile in the water on a hot day.

Ostrich: It's so hot today, crocodile. I wish I was in the water like you.

Crocodile: Come in Ostrich and try the water. You can hop on that rock.

Ostrich: I don't want to drop in the water from that rock. I can't swim.

Crocodile: I bet you can swim. Just hop in.

Ostrich: No, no, my Mom may think I'm lost. She will be cross if I hop in.

Crocodile: Pretty ostrich do hop in the water. Don't stop.

CHOP

School Bus

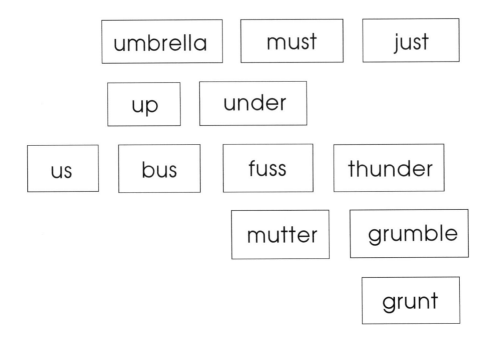

Gus and Lucy are waiting for the school bus.

Lucy: The bus is late today. Look up at the dark sky. It may rain.

Gus: I can hear thunder. Do you have an umbrella?

Lucy: If we get wet, Mom will fuss and grumble.

Gus: We must stay dry. I can hear thunder. Let's go under that tree.

Lucy: I must just check my bag again. Oh, I do have the umbrella after all.

Gus: Put up the umbrella just in time before the rain. Here comes the bus.

Trip to Disneyland

Sally and Billy are at Disneyland.

Billy: I love Disneyland.

Sally: Everything is shiny and sunny and lots of fun.

Billy: I will go on the Crazy Horse. Will you come?

Sally: I want to eat my cotton candy first. It's sticky and sweet.

Billy: After my ride I will have a big cotton candy too.

Sally: I can see Micky Mouse over there. He is funny.

Billy: Can I have some money for my ride now?

Sally: Hold on tight and don't be silly Billy.

Earthquake

shake	make	same
plate	take	awake

earthquake	grateful	safe

may	take	grace

Jake and Grace are setting by a lake.

Jake: Do you think an earthquake could happen here?

Grace: Earthquakes make everything shake.

Jake: If we were sleeping we would soon be awake.

Grace: Plates may rattle and fall.

Jake: It would take a long time to make everything the same.

Grace: I'm grateful I'm safe.

Train Trip

hailstones

rainbow	train	sailing	tail		
Aidan	Gail	railway	again	raining	pain
				rain	

Gail and Aidan are on a train.

Gail: This train goes so fast it's hard to tell we're moving.

Aidan: I like the railway. I like it more than sailing on a boat or flying in an aeroplane.

Gail: It was raining and now it's sunny. We might see a rainbow.

Aidan: Yes. Look there is a rainbow. It is on this side of the train.

Gail: Here is a dark cloud again with more rain. I can even hear hailstones.

Aidan: We're leaving the tail of the rainbow behind. What a pain.

Dreams

fleas	dream	scream		
peas	beast	feast	beat	
ice cream	tea	greasy	heat	please
eat	teasing	mean	Dean	Jean

Jean: My best dream was about a wonderful feast. I had lots of ice cream and cups of tea. I didn't have to eat peas or beans.

Dean: My worst dream was about eating peas and beans and nasty greasy food.

Jean: My worst dream had a beast with fleas in it, and it made me scream.

Dean: Please, can I tell you my best dream. My best dream is swimming in the sea and feeling clean and getting dry in the heat of the sun.

Make Believe

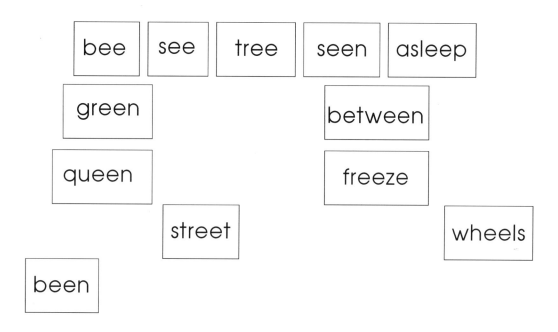

Lee and Kathleen in the land of FarAway.

Lee: Did we come here while we were asleep?

Kathleen: Do you think we have been here before?

Lee: Look at all these green things: trees, bees, and green streets between green houses.

Kathleen: Even the queen is green.

Lee: Here she comes in her car with green wheels.

Kathleen: Oh we've been seen by the queen's guard.

Lee: He is telling us to freeze. What happened next?

Valentine

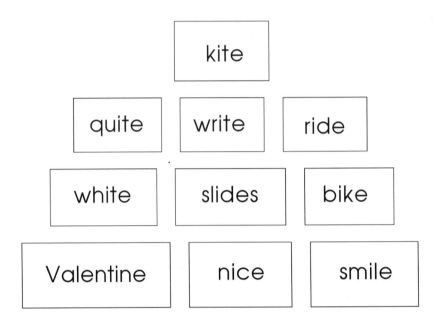

Mike and Val make Valentine poems.

Mike: Will you be my <u>Valentine</u>?
    Will you give me a <u>nice</u> <u>smile</u>?
    Will you come for a <u>bike</u> <u>ride</u>, or shall we go on the swings
    and slides?

Kathleen: I will <u>write</u> you a card.
    I will make you a <u>kite</u> and <u>tie</u> it with a <u>white</u> ribbon.
    Let's go on the <u>slides</u> together.

LONG VOWELS   o—e

Telephone Talk

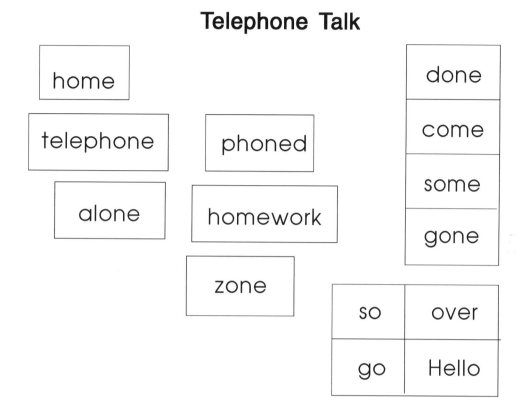

Joe is talking to Joanne on the telephone.

Joe: Hello! I'm happy you're at home.

Joanne: Hello! I'm happy you have phoned.

Joe: When will you come to see me?

Joanne: As soon as I've done some homework.

Joe: So we could play the zone game.

Joannee: Don't play alone. Go and get the game. I'll be over soon.

Two Cool Cats

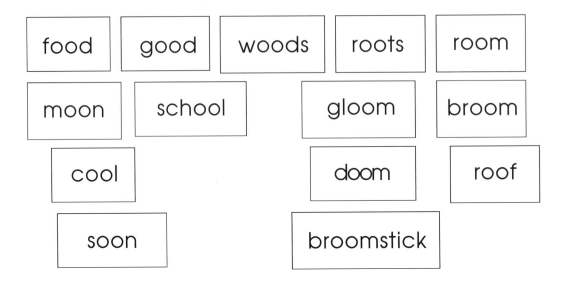

A conversation between two cats.

Cool Cat 1:   There is a full moon tonight. Let's go to the woods.

Cool Cat 2:   I want some good food tonight. I hope the moon will help us find it.

Cool Cat 1:   Let's climb this tree - over the roots and on to the branches. There's plenty of room for both of us.

Cool Cat 2:   Look over there! It's the witch's broomstick. She'll come to the woods soon tonight.

Cool Cat 1:   We'll see her take off over the roof of the school.

Cool Cat 2:   There she goes out of the gloom and doom into the sky on her broom.

Computer

computer	use	confused
blue	cute	tune
sure	clue	amusing
flute	Sue	Luke

Luke and Sue are playing on the computer.

Sue: I'm confused. How do you use this computer?

Luke: You press the blue button and it plays a cute tune.

Sue: Oh, yes. Is it a flute tune?

Luke: I'm not sure, Sue.

Sue: Now give me a clue to this game.

Luke: OK, you may find it amusing.

GROUP
SUMMARY
RECORD SHEET

NAME OF STUDENT														
AWARENESS OF WHOLE WORDS	ACT.													
AS UNITS OF SOUND (ADVANCED)	1													
	2													
	3													
	4													
	5													
RHYME (ADVANCED)														
	1													
	2													
	3													
	4													
	5													
ONSET AND RIME (ADVANCED)														
	1													
	2													
	3													
	4													
DISCRIMINATION OF MIDDLE SOUND														
	1													
	2													
	3													
	4													
	5													
	6													
	7													
	8													
	9													

GROUP
SUMMARY
RECORD SHEET
(CONTINUED)

DISCRIMINATION OF MIDDLE SOUND (CONTINUED)	ACT.											
	10											
	11											
	12											
ANALYSIS AND SYNTHESIS OF PHONEMES												
	1											
	2											
	3											
	4											
	5											
	6											
	7											
	8											
	9											
	10											
LINKAGE												
	1											
	2											
	3											
	4											
	5											
	6											
	7											
	8											
	9											

NAME OF STUDENT

GROUP
SUMMARY
RECORD SHEET
(CONTINUED)

INTEGRATION OF SOUNDS	ACT.													
	1													
	2													
	3													
	4													
	5													
	6													
	7													
	8													
	9													
	10													
	11													
	12													
	13													
	14													
	15													
	16													
	17													
	18													
	19													
	20													
	21													
PLAYS														
	1													
	2													
	3													

NAME OF STUDENT

PHONOLOGICAL AWARENESS TRAINING

STUDENT'S RECORD SHEET

NAME _____   CLASS _____

DATE STARTED _____

					COMMENTS	
AWARENESS OF WHOLE WORDS AS UNITS OF SOUND	1	2	3	4		Date Achieved
	5					
RHYME (ADVANCED)	1	2	3	4		Date Achieved
	5					
ONSET AND RIME (ADVANCED)	1	2	3	4		Date Achieved
DISCRIMINATION OF MIDDLE SOUNDS	1	2	3	4		Date Achieved
	5	6	7	8		
	9	10	11	12		
ANALYSIS AND SYNTHESIS OF PHONEMES	1	2	3	4		Date Achieved
	5	6	7	8		
	9	10				
LINKAGE	1	2	3	4		Date Achieved
	5	6	7	8		
	9					
INTEGRATION OF SOUNDS	1	2	3	4		Date Achieved
	5	6	7	8		
	9	10	11	12		
	13	14	15	16		
	17	18	19	20		
	21					

PHONOLOGICAL AWARENESS TRAINING

STUDENT'S RECORD SHEET

NAME _____   CLASS _____

DATE STARTED _____

PLAYS					COMMENTS	Date Achieved
	1	2	3	4		
	5	6	7	8		
	9	10	11	12		
	13	14				

COMMENTS